Bailey -

Joni bought [barcode] e
nature journal [barcode] ay
+ I love it!. It ren[barcode]e of
you + your walks + our time
during Covid.

I hope it helps you connect
with the Earth + stay grounded.

Happy Father's Day - you are
a great Daddy to Patches. ♡

Lots of Love,
Mom

Hi Bailey, I think you're awesome
too and hope you enjoy This
activity journal with our kind of
twist. Love you! Boat Mom

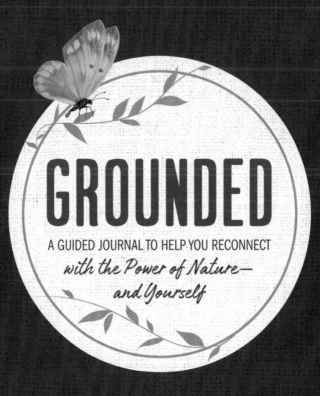

GROUNDED

A GUIDED JOURNAL TO HELP YOU RECONNECT
with the Power of Nature—
and Yourself

PATRICIA H. HASBACH, PhD

ADAMS MEDIA

NEW YORK LONDON TORONTO SYDNEY NEW DELHI

Adams media

Adams Media
An Imprint of Simon & Schuster, Inc.
100 Technology Center Drive
Stoughton, Massachusetts 02072

First Adams Media hardcover edition April 2022

ADAMS MEDIA and colophon are trademarks of
Simon & Schuster.

For information about special discounts for bulk
purchases, please contact Simon & Schuster
Special Sales at 1-866-506-1949 or business@
simonandschuster.com.

The Simon & Schuster Speakers Bureau can bring authors
to your live event. For more information or to book an event
contact the Simon & Schuster Speakers Bureau at 1-866-
248-3049 or visit our website at www. simonspeakers.com.

Produced by Indelible Editions

INDELIBLE
EDITIONS

Manufactured in China

10 9 8 7 6 5 4 3 2 1

ISBN 978-1-5072-1810-5

*This journal is dedicated
to the memory of my parents,
Robert and Dorothy Hansen,
who brought nature's wonder
and beauty into our home
every day.*

PHOTO CREDITS
COVER: 123RF.com: tandav; Shutterstock.com: Anna
Holyph; Anna Timoshenko; Apostrophe; CoffeeChocolates;
Darkdiamond67; Dionisvera; ElenaPhotos; Golovkina
Anastasia; igor kisselev; mart; Regina Bilan; Sinitsyna
.go; Venus Kaewyoo; Vladimirkarp; VolodymyrSanych.
INTERIOR: Shutterstock.com: 1001holiday, 94; aarrows,
21, 22; aarud, 5, 107; Ainalayin, 23; AlexandrBognat,
62-63; alexblacksea, 46; Alexx60, 42-43; Aliaksei Design,
4; All ForYou, 14, 123; Anastasia Lembrik, 46; Anasteisha,
42-43; AnaWhite, 88; Andrey Prokhorov, 86; Anna
Holyph, iii, 108-109; Anna Timoshenko, ii, I, 7, 12-13,
23, 44-45, 54, 66, 71, 88-89, 91, 94-95, 96-97, 102-
103, 104, 107, 108, 116-117, 123; Anzhela Sushina,
112; Apostrophe, iv, 91; asharkyu, ii, iii, 71; AVA Bitter,
56-57; basel101658, 88; bearmoney, 101; Butterfly
Hunter, 37, 54; Castro Cicero, 26-27; Cavan-Images,
114-115; CHAINFOTO24, 113; CoffeeChocolates, 104,
105; CRStocker, 44-45; Dabeygoda, 76, 77; DaMoJo, 110-
111; DavidTB, 122; Dawn Balaban, 113; Dean Penna-
la, 11; Dewin ID, 9; Dionisvera, 57; djgis, 8; Dom Uccel-
lo, 12-13; donatas1205, 1, 7, 21, 25, 39; Elena
Terletskaya, 22-23; ElenaPhotos, iv, 59; Evgeny Tomeev,
107, 112; galacticus, 72; Golovkina Anastasia, I;
GoodStudio, 96-97; Gulnara Khadeeva, 107; HAKKI
ARSLAN, 16-17; HappyPictures, 12; Hein Nouwens,
66-67, 78, 79; Helen Lane, 90-91; HN Works, 78;
iamaimmy, 116; igor kisselev, 4; ImHope, 54-55; In Art,
119; irin-k, 68; Irina Rogova, 107; Irish_design, 77;
irmairma, 10; Iryn, 96-97; itim2101, 48; ivleva1975,
32; Jan-Kalle Jonath, 77; jaylopez, 86-87; Johnny
Adolphson, 61; ju_see, 33; kapona, 47; Katerina
Kashera, 71; Katerina Shvarts, 70-71; Katong, 37, 69,
120-121; kikk, 38-39; Konstantin Remizov, 37, 124;
kostrez, 18; Kudryashka, 4; le adhiz, 40; Leszek Czerwonka,
48; lilac, 89; Lili Wave, 28; logika600, 119; Margie
Hurwich, 30; mart, 4; MeSamong, 48-49; N8Allen, 53;
nadezhda F, 20; Nastina, 44, 45; natrot, 1, 3, 67, 20-
21, 24-25, 78-79, 118-119; Nudphon Phuengsuwan,
74-75; Olga_Angelloz, 46; One Pixel Studio, 49;
Patrick Daxenbichler, 36; Pavlo S, 64-65; photka, 15;
Picsfive, 37, 81; Regina Bilan, 4; RinaArt21, 102; Ryan
DeBerardinis, 109; SakSa, 85; sema srinouljan, 50;
Shark_749, 58-59; shopplaywood, 24; Sunset And
Sea Design, 62-63; sunwart, 107; svrid79, 104;
Tamiris6, 112-113; TB studio, 116-117; Thirteen, 113;
TierneyMJ, 108; tn-prints, 46; Tolchik, 98-99; TopGear,
91; Transia Design, 58-59; TwoMine, 97; ulia_color, 89;
Undrey, 120-121; valkoinen, iv, 107, 128; Valumyan,
120-121; Vector FX, 78,79; Vector Point Studio, 80-81;
Vivid Image VI, 118; Vladimir Prusakov, 107; Vladimirkarp,
ii, 2; Volodymyr Burdiak, 82; wannawit_vck, 94-95;
Wiktoria Matynia, 79; yod 67, 28, 29; Yuliya Koldovska, 51.

Contents

1 Introduction
2 Early Childhood Memory
3 Favorite View from My Home
4 Display a Nature Collection
6 Inner and Outer Connection
9 The Water Cycle and You
10 Color the World: Waves
12 Grow a Windowsill Herb Garden
14 Cooking Over Fire
15 Gathering Around the Grill
16 Early-Morning Meditation
19 Nature Reminds Us of Our Resilience
20 A Flower's Beauty
24 Where Do I Live?
28 Love Your Pet
31 Splash!
32 Color the World: Raindrops
34 Screen-Time and Nature-Time Log
38 Clouds in the Sky
40 My Nature Gift of the Day
42 Standing Under the Shower
44 Meditation on a Tangerine
46 Nature's Symphony
48 Workspace Restoration
51 It's in the Details!
52 The Landscape of Childhood
55 Color the World: Butterflies
56 Sense of Place
58 Observing the Night Sky
60 Sitting Fireside
62 Preparing Your Sleep Space
65 Your Nature Mentor

66 Gratitude: A Tool for Coping with Stress
69 Looking for Nature's Patterns
70 Color the World: Fractals
72 By the Light of the Moon
74 Open the Windows
76 Scents of the Seasons
78 Recapturing a Primal Skill
80 Growing Houseplants
82 Tune into Your Favorite Webcam
83 The Sound of Water
84 Creepy Crawlies
86 Listening to Nature's Night Noises
88 Our Feathered Friends
90 Color the World: Flowers
92 Build a Fort Indoors
94 Capturing Nature's Beauty
97 Cooking as a Sensual, Sacred Art
98 Basking in the Sun
100 Soaking Your Feet
102 My Time and Life Satisfaction
104 Making Leaf and Flower Art
106 Bring Nature's Colors and Beauty Inside
108 Are You Feeling Ecoanxiety?
110 Befriend a Tree
112 My Special Nature Object
114 Evening Meditation
116 What Is Your Resilience Style?
118 Discover Your Totem
120 Reciprocity

Relax by heading outside to appreciate the warmth of the sun. Feel your heart rate slow when sitting by the fire and enjoying the company of loved ones. Find peace in a quiet afternoon spent watching and sketching the cloud formations you see.

Introduction

We know deep within us that contact with nature is good for our psychological and physical health. A mountain of scientific evidence confirms that it reduces stress, relieves attention fatigue, eases depression and anxiety, and fosters creativity. Interacting with the living world can ground us, offer a sense of security and belonging, deepen the roots of our resilience, and enhance our sensory awareness that contributes to feeling fully alive. After all, we are nature! As a species, we evolved as part of the natural world.

But at no time in our species' history have we been more removed from it. Research shows that people who report strong connectedness to nature are happier and more likely to report feeling that life is worthwhile . . . so when (and how) do we find the time to integrate nature into our busy lives?

Inspired by the practice of ecotherapy, a method of treatment that recognizes the healing benefits of interactions with nature, this journal provides an inviting space for you to reflect on how you can engage more intentionally with nature where you live in order to form deeper and more meaningful bonds with the natural world. *Grounded: A Guided Journal to Help You Reconnect with the Power of Nature—and Yourself* invites you to create some of these essential interactions in your daily life and offers ways to easily incorporate nearby nature into your home, including:

Displaying a collection of found objects, such as shells or rocks • Growing low-maintenance houseplants in your workspace • Starting a windowsill herb garden to brighten up your kitchen • Befriending a nearby tree • And many more!

In addition to journal prompts, you'll find beautiful art and illustrations, inspirational quotes, and surprising findings from scientific research, as well as additional resources to expand your experience. Your creativity will be tapped with suggestions for drawings, and you'll relax while coloring beautifully outlined nature art.

Learn to engage your senses, decrease your screen time, and even foster a sense of nature connectedness by emphasizing the sensory-rich world around you with prompts and activities that remind you of your connection to something larger than yourself.

Early Childhood Memory

Our love of nature is often spawned in our early childhood experiences. What's one of your early memories of interacting with nature? Were you in the forest, at the beach, in your backyard? Was anyone else with you? What do you remember feeling then? What are you feeling now as you recall this memory?

Use the space below to record your memories.

Nature's ongoing presence offers many of us a sense of security through the ebbs and flows of life.

Favorite View from My Home

Looking out the window is one of the most common ways we interact with nature. Do you have a favorite window with a view of the outdoors?

What do you love most about that view? What draws your attention?

Is there anything you can do to make it easier for you to relax and enjoy this spot, such as changing a window covering or creating a cozy sitting nook?

Find yourself flagging at work? Take a minute to look out the window. Studies show that the restorative benefits of contact with nature relax our "directed attention," which can be exhausted by our daily usage of screens and concentrated focus on our work.

Display a Nature Collection

Many of us enjoy collecting objects from nature, such as rocks, feathers, seashells, tree bark, or sea glass. These items can conjure memories of a special place, an enjoyable vacation, or time spent with special people in our lives. These collections can also remind us of the beauty in the natural world and can bring the bigger world into our home.

4

Do you have a collection of nature objects? Reflect on the memories connected with your collection.

Is your collection displayed in a way that you can enjoy it on a regular basis, or is it tucked away in a drawer? Here are a few suggestions for making your nature objects more prominent in your home:

Fill a small fish bowl with seashells. • Line a window ledge with sea glass to catch the sunlight. • Fill a small basket with rocks or set a few favorite rocks next to your computer.

Inner and Outer Connection

Ecopsychology is the study of the human-nature relationship, with the core assumption that our inner world and the outer world are intimately connected.

An example of how the outer world affects our inner world is the sadness and grief we feel when a beloved landscape is destroyed by fire. Another example is the profound joy we experience while witnessing a baby animal take its first steps.

Describe a meaningful moment you've had in nature.

There are also times when the outer landscape seems to reflect what we're feeling inside. For example, the dark sky before a storm may reflect our mood on a bad day. The cool, fresh wind on a spring day might reflect the excitement of a new beginning in our lives.

Draw a landscape that reflects what emotions you are feeling today.

The Water Cycle and You

Water is the essence of life! Approximately 70 percent of the Earth consists of water, but only about 2.5 percent of it is fresh water. When you pour yourself a tall glass of cool, refreshing water, reflect on your gratitude for this life-giving, life-sustaining element of nature.

Have you ever wondered where your water comes from when you turn on the tap? Maybe you picture the water treatment facility in your community, but what journey did the water take to get to you? Did it originate in a mountain snowpack or forest stream? Was it a cloud formed in the winds over an ocean?

Use the space here to record the imagined journey this water traveled to get to you.

You can learn more about the source of your water through interactive maps published by the Environmental Protection Agency at EPA.gov/waterdata/hows-my-waterway.

"No man ever steps in the same river twice, for it's not the same river and he's not the same man."

—Heraclitus, Greek philosopher

Grow a Windowsill Herb Garden

Herbs delight our sense of smell and taste and bring varied textures and color to a windowsill garden, which can be one of the most cheerful and relaxing parts of your home. Nothing is as satisfying as clipping a few sprigs of an herb you've grown to add flavor to a dish. Some herbs, like rosemary and basil, release their aromatic oils when we touch them, leaving a delightful smell in the air and on your hands.

Your local nursery or farmers' market can help you select easy care options with similar needs for light, humidity, and temperature. Here are a few suggestions:

PARSLEY is a bright green, nutrient-rich herb that is easy to grow. It can be used fresh or dried in a variety of dishes.

ROSEMARY resembles a miniature fir tree with its dark green, needlelike leaves. In the spring, it develops pretty blue blossoms along the branches. Rosemary is thought to strengthen memory; in ancient Greece, students would weave rosemary sprigs into their hair while studying for exams.

BASIL has bright, shiny, oval, green leaves and develops small white flowers in midsummer. It has a sweet aromatic smell and a strong flavor that pairs well with tomatoes in any form.

Sketch your ideas of what herbs you'd like to grow.

MINT has a cool, refreshing taste and smell and comes in a variety of flavors. Try putting a few leaves into your ice tea or pouring hot water over a sprig to make a cup of mint tea.

CHIVES look like wild onions with thin blades that can grow to a foot tall and develop a pretty, edible, purple bloom in early summer.

13

Cooking Over Fire

Cooking over fire is a primal human-nature interaction that sets our ancestors apart from our animal kin. Something about that experience still feels magical, with the sound of the crackling wood, the beauty of stars twinkling as the sky darkens, and the taste of food prepared intentionally.

Have you ever cooked over an open fire? If so, do you recall feeling the cool air on your back while your face was warmed by the flames? Or the smell of the food cooking and the smoke in your hair?

Take some time to reflect on your experiences of cooking outdoors. If you haven't cooked over an open fire, describe how you imagine it would feel.

Gathering Around the Grill

Today, most of us don't cook dinner over an open fire unless we're on a camping trip. A more domestic version of this human-nature interaction is grilling on a patio or deck or in a local park. Whether we're roasting wild-caught salmon over an open flame or grilling burgers above a bed of glowing coals on the backyard patio, our thoughts inevitably go to those with whom we've shared the experience.

Describe your experience of enjoying a meal cooked outdoors with the people in your life.

Early-Morning Meditation

Sunrise offers us stable grounding in what can sometimes feel like an unpredictable world. Each day's awakening offers a new opportunity for starting fresh, setting intentions, and reconnecting with what is most important to us.

Choose a morning to rise with the sun. Find a place where you can observe the slow illumination of the sky, feel the cool damp air on your skin, hear the conversing of birds, and smell the freshness of the early-morning air. Try to avoid thinking about the day to come and be fully present to experience the dawn of a new day.

Sunrise is a powerful time to journal about new beginnings, hopes, and dreams. If you could do anything today, without limitations, what would you do? Write about your early-morning reflections.

"The wondrous diverse beauty of the natural world remains the source of who we are and can become as individuals and societies."

—Stephen R. Kellert, author of *Birthright*

Nature Reminds Us of Our Resilience

Every year, wildfire transforms green forests into blackened landscapes. After witnessing the devastation, it can be common to think that everything is lost. But did you know that some plants only release seeds and sprout after exposure to fire? The layers of ash enrich the soil, and allow more sunlight to reach the forest floor, enabling growth. A forest's recovery from fire is an example of nature's resilience.

Life is not always easy. Most of us have suffered some trauma, sadness, loss, or pain. When we have survived a difficult time, we might look back and admire our resilience, thinking, "If I survived that, I can survive anything."

Write about an event that changed your life but allowed for new growth and more confidence and strength than you thought possible.

A Flower's Beauty

Sending flowers to celebrate a special occasion, cheer someone up, and express our condolences does more than beautify the surroundings. Flowers touch a deep part of us associated with survival, as flowers grow only where water is found.

People in the Victorian era assigned meanings to flowers so they could convey unspoken feelings when given. A white lily was sent to say "my love is pure," while a yellow pansy meant "thinking of you."

Do you have a favorite flower? If so, what does it mean to you? Are there specific memories or reflections associated with it?

Place a beautiful flower in front of you. Take time to really look at it. Notice the intricacies of the petals, leaves, and stem. Determine what about it appeals to you—perhaps its color, its symmetry, its structure, its imperfections?

In the space below, draw, sketch, or paint the flower. Don't worry about being artistic. Just try to express how its beauty makes you feel.

"If we could see the miracle of a single flower clearly, our whole life would change."

—Jack Kornfield, author of *Buddha's Little Instruction Book*

Where Do I Live?

With our increased dependence on GPS, most of us no longer intuitively understand where we are in the world. Orienting ourselves within our homes can be grounding and provide a sense of belonging to a place. In the Northern Hemisphere, the sun rises in the east and sets in the west, which provides a basic orientation of the four cardinal directions.

Find a place in your home where you can see the sun emerge from the skyline in the morning. Similarly, look for where you can see the last sliver of the sun's light in the evening. You might have to step outside to get a clear understanding of the position of the sun as it moves east to west each day. This predictable journey across the sky can provide a sense of security and a visual cue to our position in the world.

Notice what parts of your home are illuminated by the sun's rays at various times of the day. With what you know about the sun's path, try to determine whether the sunlight comes from north, south, east, or west. Also, reflect on your own sense of direction: Is it something that comes naturally to you? Or is finding your way sometimes challenging?

Imagine having a bird's-eye view of your home and the surrounding area. Draw what the world looks like around your home.

You can further orient
yourself by finding the
latitude and longitude
of your home using
Google Maps.

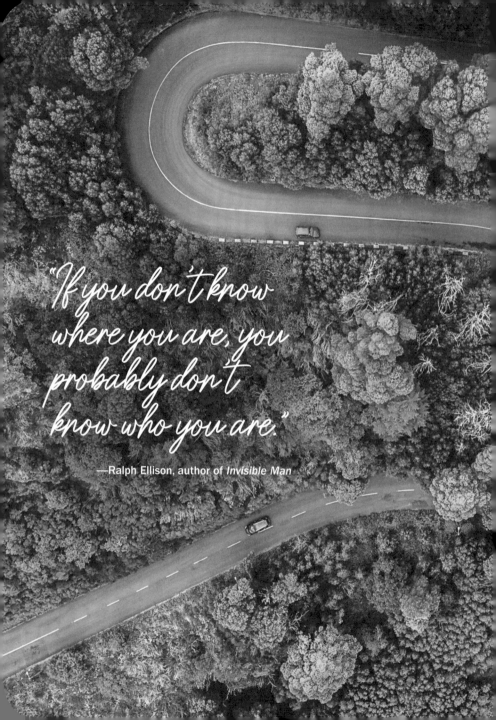

"If you don't know where you are, you probably don't know who you are."

—Ralph Ellison, author of *Invisible Man*

Love Your Pet

What is more welcoming than a dog that greets you bouncing with excitement when you come home? Or maybe it's a cat that purrs contentedly and rubs against your ankles when you arrive. Interactions with our furry family members bring joy, a sense of being needed, unconditional love, and contentment.

If you have a furry family member, take some time to notice how you feel when you share time with your pet—stroking their fur, playing a game, romping outdoors, taking a walk, or curling up on the couch.

What is your favorite time together with your pet?

_____

_____

_____

_____

_____

_____

_____

_____

_____

_____

_____

For many people, animal companions are essential to their happiness. Numerous studies have shown that having pets might be associated with improved mental and physical health, including reducing stress and anxiety, lowering heart rate and blood pressure, and promoting social interaction.

If you don't have a pet at home, did you have one earlier in life? If so, what do you remember most about that pet?

_____

_____

_____

_____

_____

_____

_____

_____

If you could pet any animal without being harmed, which would you choose? What do you imagine it would feel like?

_____

_____

_____

_____

_____

_____

_____

_____

Splash!

Nothing is as refreshing on a hot day as splashing your face with water from a cold lake. It's a primal act that humans have engaged in since the beginning of time. At home, we can refresh ourselves in a similar fashion by cupping our hands under the faucet and splashing our face with cool water from the tap. Try it!

How do you feel? Does splashing your face or sipping water from your hands bring up any memories for you?

_____

_____

_____

_____

_____

_____

_____

_____

_____

_____

_____

_____

Japanese gardens often have water flowing over bamboo into a basin right outside the temple grounds for washing one's hands before entering. Architectural features like this one intended to facilitate interactions between people and nature elements are called biophilic design. Can you imagine adding a water feature like this outside your home?

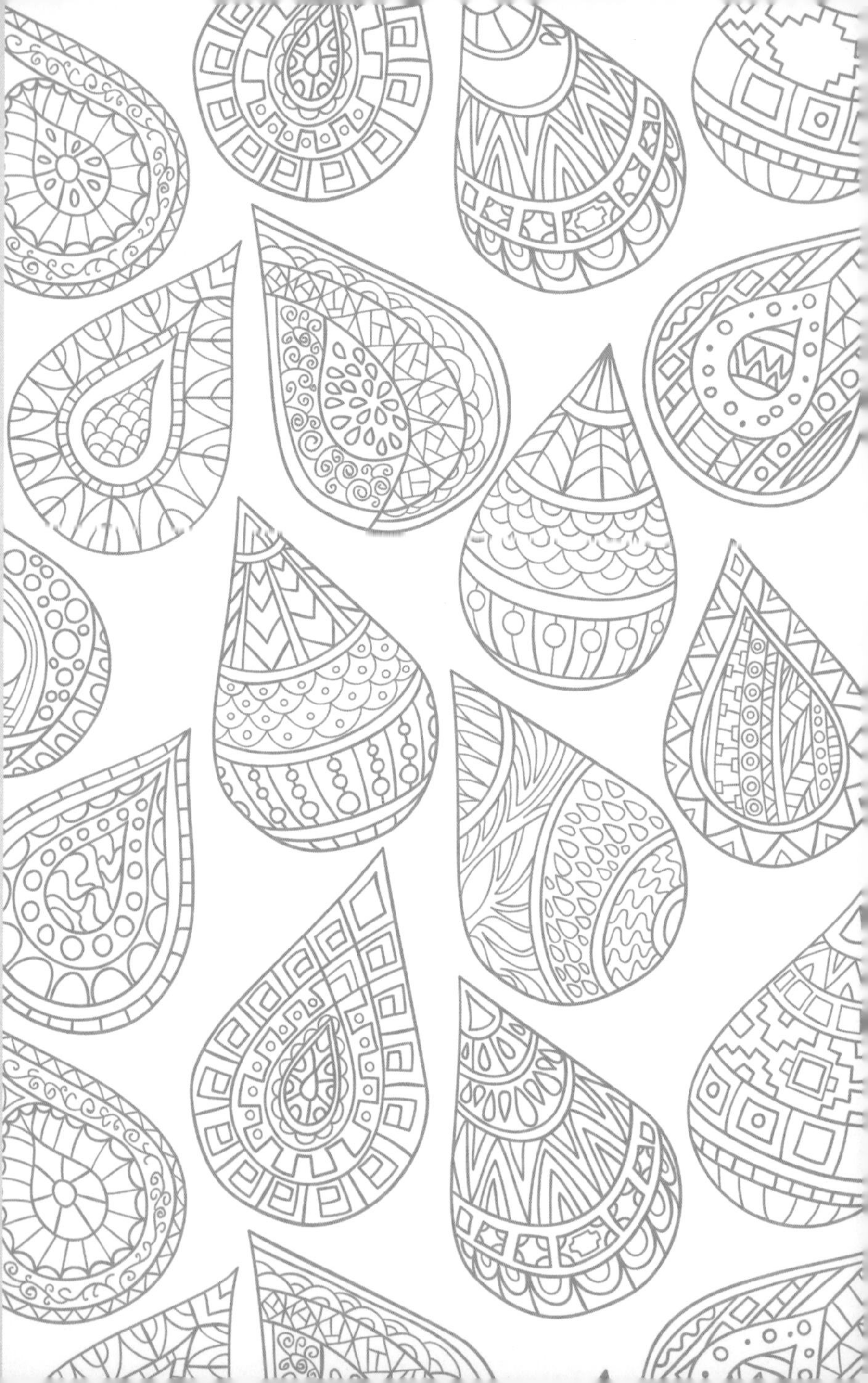

"Some people
feel the rain:
others just
get wet."

—Roger Miller, songwriter

Screen-Time and Nature-Time Log

During the last decade, people have been spending more time engaged with some sort of screen and less time outdoors with nature. According to a 2019 Nielsen report, the average adult spent eleven and a half hours each day consuming media. That same year, a study out of Stanford University showed that a forty-five-minute walk in nearby nature can improve mood, creativity, and working memory.

To raise awareness of your screen time and nature time, consider keeping a log for seven days. Record the date, type of digital technology you're interacting with (TV, computer, cell phone, tablet, etc.), the activity (work, school, entertainment, communication with family or friends, gaming), and the amount of time spent with your screen. For the same period, record the time you spend outdoors in nature, noting the date, location, activity, and amount of time spent.

DATE	TECHNOLOGY USED	ACTIVITY	AMOUNT OF TIME

SCREEN TIME

	DATE	LOCATION	ACTIVITY	AMOUNT OF TIME
NATURE TIME				

Without judgment, summarize what you see as you analyze your screen-time and nature-time log. What do you notice? What are you happy with? What would you like to modify?

"The more high tech our lives become, the more nature we need."

—Richard Louv, author of *The Nature Principle*

Clouds in the Sky

Staring at a computer screen or other work-related task for too long can leave us feeling exhausted. Overworking our *directed attention* can lead to cognitive fatigue, confusion, and brain fog.

We can relax our minds by turning our gazes to elements in nature that provide *soft fascination.* For example, watching clouds move across the sky provides the opportunity to activate our *involuntary attention*, which allows our minds to relax. It can also stimulate imagination while providing clues about the weather.

Go outside, lie down in the soft grass or sit on your deck or patio, and look up. If you can't go outdoors, find a window or skylight where you can get a clear view of the sky. For at least fifteen minutes, notice the cloud formations and movements above you. How would you describe them? Let your imagination kick in. What do the clouds resemble? Continue to watch how the clouds change shape. Do you remember doing this as a child?

Reflect on the questions above and note how you felt differently from the beginning to the end of the exercise.

Draw the cloud formations you observed.

My Nature Gift of the Day

We can connect more deeply with the natural world by being more intentional about noticing how we interact with it every day. When we set our minds to really experience the sights, sounds, and smells of nature around us, we experience so much more!

One way to foster our intention is to look for your "nature gift of the day." It might be an unexpected rainbow that appears after a rain shower, the melodious song of a wren outside your window, or the glistening of the first snowfall in the moonlight.

In the space below, write down your "nature gift of the day" for each day of the coming week.

Sunday:

Monday:

Tuesday:

Wednesday:

Thursday:

Friday:

Saturday:

After one week of intentionally looking for your "nature gift of the day," did you find that you noticed more nature around you? Do you see yourself continuing this intentional practice? How did this practice increase your sense of gratitude for the natural world?

Standing Under the Shower

After a long day, few things feel better than standing in the shower and allowing the warm streams of water to wash away the stress of the day. This everyday experience simulates a wilder human-nature interaction of standing beneath falling water.

When you step into the shower this evening, heighten your experience by imagining that you are standing under a beautiful waterfall. Close your eyes and notice how the water feels on your skin. Listen to the sound of the water's flow. Taste the water on your tongue. Breathe in the damp, warm air. Feel your shoulders relax under the rush.

Did you experience this shower differently than your usual shower? What happens when you are intentional and in the present?

_____

_____

_____

_____

_____

_____

_____

_____

_____

_____

_____

_____

_____

Meditation on a Tangerine

In our fast-paced, modern world, life can sometimes feel rushed and out of control. Practicing mindfulness helps us slow our thoughts in order to regain a sense of peace and centeredness. Most mindfulness practices begin by focusing on our breath and call us to be completely present in the here and now. The following exercise, based on a meditation by the Zen master, spiritual leader, and author Thich Nhat Hanh, extends the focus from our breath to our senses of sight, smell, taste, and touch. You will need a tangerine or any piece of fruit that you enjoy.

1.
Find a comfortable place to sit. Take a few deep breaths, noticing the air flowing in and out of your body. Allow your thoughts and body to quiet.

2.
Place the tangerine in the palm of your hand and think about its origins. You might find yourself visualizing the tangerine tree standing in the sunlight and being showered by the rain.

3.
Slowly peel the tangerine. Notice what the flesh feels like in your hands. Notice the mist and fragrance that burst forth. Begin to break apart the sections of the fruit. What do you notice?

4.
When you're ready, bring one section to your mouth and take a slow, mindful bite, noticing the texture, taste, and smell. Feel the juice flow over your tongue. Allow yourself the time to enjoy the remaining sections.

What new features did you notice about the fruit? About your state of mind? About your senses? About your breath?

_____

_____

_____

_____

_____

_____

_____

_____

_____

_____

_____

_____

_____

_____

Often we eat without thinking or even fully tasting what we put into our mouth. Taking the time to fully enjoy our food is good for our digestion, connects us with the bigger world, and fosters our sense of gratitude and well-being.

Nature's Symphony

Every day, a symphony is playing right outside your window! Early
morning and dusk are great times to hear the activities of birds,
insects, frogs, and other creatures in the natural world.

Sit for a moment and close your eyes. Notice the sounds of the wind
and the rustling of trees and shrubs and grass. Listen for sounds that are close by and
ones that seem far off as well. Imagine the sounds are part of a symphonic orchestra. Are
there repeated refrains?

You will hear human-made sounds as well. How do they fit into the symphony?

Try this activity at different times of the year and at different times of the day. Notice
how the symphony changes with various weather conditions.

What sounds stood out to you most? Write a review of the symphony you heard.

_____

_____

_____

_____

_____

_____

_____

_____

_____

_____

_____

_____

_____

_____

_____

_____

_____

_____

_____

_____

_____

_____

Workspace Restoration

In our technologically focused world, many of us find that success at work means staring at a computer all day, trying not to get distracted from the task at hand. But this single-minded focus can lead to cognitive fatigue, which can actually make us more susceptible to distraction and decrease our ability to filter out irrelevant information. Studies show that natural environments help diminish cognitive fatigue by offering "soft" fascination, such as leaves rustling in the wind, which promotes attention restoration. So, what can you do to invite nature into your workspace?

What ideas do you have to "green" your workspace?

Here are a few ideas to consider: Potted plants near a computer have been shown to reduce eye strain and fatigue. • Photos of nature posted nearby can "take you away" and provide visual relief. • Elements such as rocks, shells, and feathers can provide natural textures and foster memories of where they were collected. • Earth tones and natural colors can provide a calming environment.

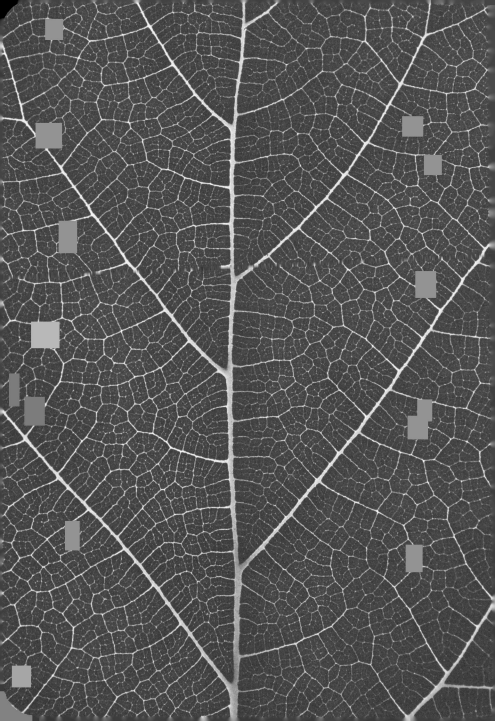

It's in the Details!

Focusing on a flower blossom or the bark of a tree or a twelve-inch patch of grass for a short spell can help bring the wonder and beauty of nature into your day. If you're able to go outdoors for this exercise, please do. Notice what draws your attention. If you aren't able to go outside, find a houseplant, rock, or even the wood furniture or floorboards in your home.

Take a moment to focus on what you see. After observing the object for about thirty seconds, move closer, cutting the distance in half. If you're standing, you might bend down on one knee. Notice how you see it differently. After another thirty seconds, cut the distance in half again. What do you see now that you hadn't noticed at first? Finally, get as close as possible to the item and see the details.

Now step back to the original position from which you first observed the item. What do you notice now? Do you feel differently toward it?

The Landscape of Childhood

Where did you grow up? Would you describe it as rural, small town, suburban, or city? What natural features were nearby? Where did you play as a child? Were you free to roam, or did you have more confined boundaries? Were there animals present? What kind of weather did you experience? What is most memorable about the place you grew up?

Use these questions to describe a scene from your childhood.

"The landscape of childhood becomes an indelible part of memory. You absorb it. it absorbs you."

—Diane Ackerman, author of *Cultivating Delight*

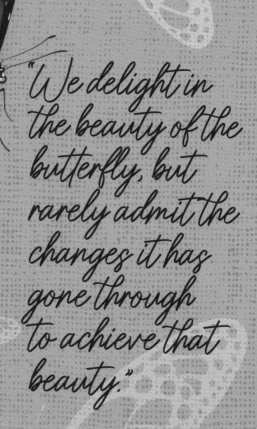

"We delight in the beauty of the butterfly, but rarely admit the changes it has gone through to achieve that beauty."

—Maya Angelou, poet

Sense of Place

Thanks to our evolutionary history, humans show a preference for savanna-like landscapes. We're wired to like places with a flat expanse of land for easy viewing of predators, a shelter of trees for refuge, and a source of water, all of which kept our early ancestors alive. Studies show that modern adults also prefer landscapes that are familiar to us, such as the places where we grew up or lived much of our lives.

What kind of landscape do you prefer? Mountains with trees and water, deserts with rocks, rolling hills of open space, meadows at a forest's edge, or more sculpted landscapes dotted with human-built environments, such as cityscapes or suburbs? In what landscape do you feel most at home?

In the space below, describe the elements of a landscape that contribute to your sense of place.

Sketch your preferred landscape.

Observing the Night Sky

Looking up at the velvety night sky can be a profound experience. The vastness of the universe, the mystery of the unknown, and the beauty of the shimmering stars can instill feelings of humility, awe, and gratitude. Observing the night sky might also conjure childhood memories of camping trips or backyard sleepovers.

If you're able, go outside and lie down in the grass or get comfortable on a patio chaise lounge. If you can't go outdoors, find a window or skylight where you can get a view of the night sky. Turn off any lights inside. Notice what captures your attention first. If it's a clear night, notice the obvious stars. Then look deep, noticing the fainter twinkles of light. Let your eyes adjust. Keep looking.

Do you notice anything that surprises you? What words describe how you feel as you look at the night sky?

_____

_____

_____

_____

_____

_____

_____

_____

_____

_____

_____

Sitting Fireside

Sitting near fire is one of the earliest human-nature interactions. Our early ancestors gathered there to share the events of the day, to reveal the dreams of the night, and to tell stories that shaped the lives of the listeners.

In our modern world, you might have a fireplace in your home or a candle grouping set up on the coffee table or hearth. Perhaps you have a firepit in your yard or a propane fire table on the patio. Whatever the setup, sitting by a small fire invites relaxation and intimacy. There is something magical about watching the dance of the flames and feeling their warmth.

Remember a time when you were sitting by the fire with a loved one, family members, a group of friends, or a community of people. What stories were told? What do you remember most? If you haven't had the experience of sitting by a fire, what do you imagine it would be like?

"Sometimes a person needs a story more than food to stay alive."

—Barry Lopez, author of *Crow and Weasel*

Preparing Your Sleep Space

We spend roughly one-third of our time in our bedrooms, so spending time intentionally preparing your sleep space is a beautiful gift to give yourself. How do you make this space inviting, calming, healing, and restorative?

Research from environmental psychology confirms what we already know: certain smells, colors, and amenities contribute to a restorative night's sleep. Scents like lavender have been shown to contribute to relaxation. Soft, muted wall colors promote a serene landscape that feels calm. Temperatures on the cool side generally aid people in sleeping deeper. Cozy bedding where you can "cocoon" helps you feel snug and secure. Uncluttered space also makes a room more peaceful.

Look at your bedroom. What do you find most calming and restful? What would you most like to change about your sleep space to make it feel more restorative? What is one small thing you can add or remove from your sleep space right now?

"If a child is to keep alive his inborn sense of wonder . . . he needs the companionship of at least one adult who can share it, rediscovering with him the joy, excitement and mystery of the world we live in."

—Rachel Carson, author of *The Sense of Wonder*

Your Nature Mentor

Who introduced you to the natural world? Researchers interviewed environmentalists in the United States and Norway to determine the sources of their commitment to the natural world. Most of them described spending extended time outdoors as children with adults who taught them to love and respect nature.

What memories do you have of spending time outdoors with a special adult? What are you most grateful for about that time?

_____

_____

_____

_____

_____

_____

_____

_____

_____

_____

_____

_____

_____

_____

_____

_____

Gratitude: A Tool for Coping with Stress

Chronic stress keeps your nervous system on high alert. If you don't have an outlet for that stress, over time it leads to feeling drained and in a brain fog. It also puts you at risk for a variety of health issues, including heart disease and inflammation, and it may contribute to depression, anxiety, and sleep issues.

Keeping a gratitude journal can be a great way to regain perspective when you're stressed. One way to foster that feeling is to mindfully appreciate the natural world for each breath we take, each drop of water we drink, and each bite of food we consume. Start here with three things in nature you're feeling especially grateful for today:

1.

2.

3.

During stressful times, coping suggestions include:
- *Get regular exercise*
- *Eat a healthy diet*
- *Get outdoors regularly*
- *Limit news consumption*
- *Engage in a hobby*
- *Spend time with trusted loved ones*
- *Laughter*
- *Extend compassion to yourself*

What does it take to refill your tank when you feel depleted? What natural elements are most relaxing to you?

In the coming week, write one thing each day that you're grateful for.

Sunday:

Monday:

Tuesday:

Wednesday:

Thursday:

Friday:

Saturday:

" *There is no better designer than nature.*"

—Alexander McQueen, designer

Looking for Nature's Patterns

Humans are attracted to beauty in nature that is rich in detail and diversity, while simultaneously ordered and organized. This quality of organized complexity is known as fractal geometry. Fractals are patterns found in nature where the parts reflect the whole. The basic patterns are similar to one another but not identical. Examples of fractal patterns in nature include snowflakes, leaves on a tree, the fiddleheads of a fern, lightning bolts, river deltas, and the spiral of a shell. Architectural features such as stained-glass windows and designs for fabrics and wallpaper often incorporate fractal patterns. Take a look around your home and see if you can identify natural or human-made objects that include fractal patterns.

Draw a fractal pattern that you found in your home.

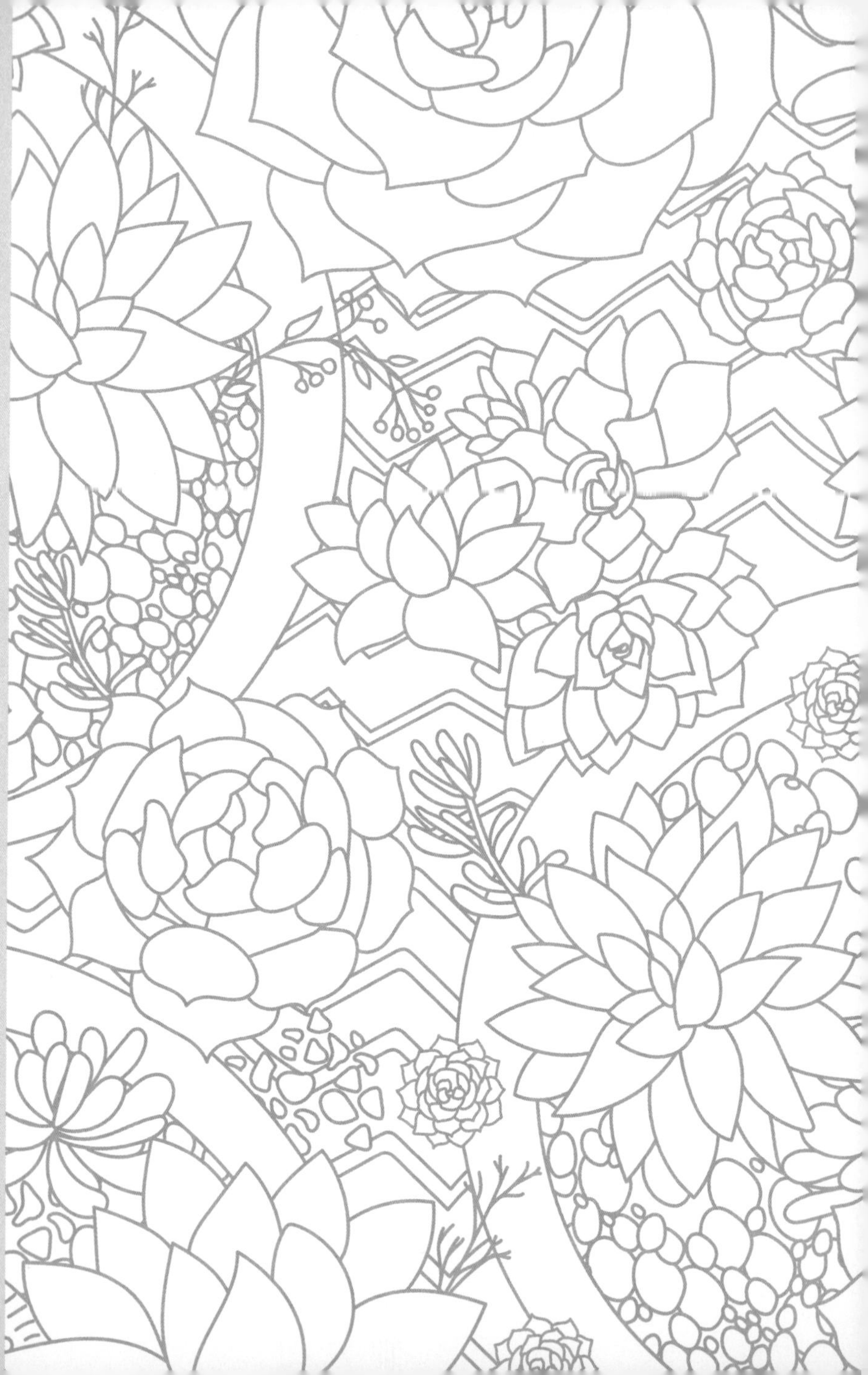

"Those who dwell . . . among the beauties and mysteries of the Earth are never alone or weary of life . . . There is something infinitely healing in the repeated refrains of nature."

—Rachel Carson, author of *Silent Spring*

By the Light of the Moon

Some nights, the moon looks like a bright disk in the sky, while others it appears as a sliver of silvery white light or isn't visible at all. These changes in appearance are called the phases of the moon. As the moon travels around the Earth, it cycles through eight distinct phases that determine, from our perspective, how much of the moon is illuminated. Surrounded by myth and mystery, the moon captivates our imagination, controls the tides of the oceans, and influences the inner tides of our body. The word *menstruation* traces back to the word for moon. The predictable monthly phases of the moon can provide us with a deep sense of belonging to something bigger than ourselves, and they can inspire awe and humility.

As you look up at the moon, what feelings are aroused? What memories come up for you related to the light of the moon? What questions do you have?

Open the Windows

Let the air into your home! The breeze can give clues to the weather and can influence how you feel emotionally.

Sit by an open window or door.

- Close your eyes and notice how the air feels on your skin.
- How does the air smell? Notice if it's cold or warm as you breathe.
- What sounds do you hear being carried by the wind? Birdsong? Human-made sounds? Leaves rustling? Water flowing? Wind chimes ringing?
- Take a moment to notice your own breath. Is it full and deep or light and shallow? What does it feel like to take a few deep breaths?
- What is different about breathing the outside air versus the indoor air? As you focus your awareness on the breeze and your breath, do you feel more alive?
- Keeping your eyes closed, notice if you feel a connection between the wind and your breath.
- Now open your eyes, look outside, and notice what draws your attention.

What movements do you observe? Is the wind a powerful force today? You might try this exercise at various times of the year and at various times of the day.

_____

_____

_____

_____

_____

_____

_____

_____

_____

_____

_____

_____

_____

_____

_____

_____

_____

_____

_____

Scents of the Seasons

Certain smells from seasons past rekindle childhood memories. Science tells us that smell was the first of our senses to develop, and it has a profound influence on our memories. For example, the scent of pine might stir memories of the Christmas holiday and the winter solstice, or the sweet smell of lilacs might remind us of the early days of spring.

What scents do you associate with the seasons of the year?

What feelings come up for you as you remember the smells of the seasons? What memories are awakened?

_____

_____

_____

_____

_____

_____

_____

_____

_____

_____

_____

_____

Recapturing a Primal Skill

With our busy, fast-paced lives, we've outsourced many skills that previous generations practiced regularly. Maybe it is grinding wheat and baking bread, picking berries and making jam, planting a vegetable garden and canning the harvest, or spinning wool into yarn and knitting a hat. Perhaps it involves learning to forage for mushrooms or learning to fly fish. Many of these sensory-rich activities involve interacting with elements of nature.

Did your parents or grandparents have a skill that involved nature elements which you've thought about trying? Who did this activity and what are your memories of helping them with the task? What are ways you might bring that activity into your life?

_____

_____

_____

_____

_____

_____

_____

_____

_____

_____

_____

_____

_____

_____

_____

_____

Growing Houseplants

Indoor plants beautify our home, help cleanse the air, and offer the opportunity for us to care for them. The act of tending for another being—even a single houseplant—answers a deep desire that humans have to be needed.

Studies show that when indoor plants are present in an office space, workers report greater job satisfaction and have fewer sick days. Similarly, when potted plants are present in a patient's hospital room, the patient requires less pain medication and goes home sooner.

You can green your home workspace or brighten your kitchen windowsill with easy-to-grow houseplants. Local nurseries and home-and-garden stores can suggest plants that will thrive in all sorts of conditions. Some online vendors will even ship a houseplant to you with easy-to-follow directions included for its care.

Where would you like to add more greenery in your home?

_____

_____

_____

_____

_____

_____

_____

_____

_____

_____

_____

Draw a houseplant you'd like to take care of in your home.

Tune into Your Favorite Webcam

Webcams are an amazing way to view nature remotely. Whether we're watching a feeding station for birds in the rain forests of Panama, a redtail hawk nest in New York City, wildlife visiting a watering hole in South Africa, or the ebb and flow of the tides at a favorite beach, technology brings faraway nature into our homes and sparks curiosity and wonder.

Research suggests that virtual nature, though not as powerful as real nature interaction, offers some benefits in stress reduction and stress recovery.

Take some time to tune into an online webcam. Maybe revisit a beloved vacation spot or one you yearn to explore. Which webcam did you choose to visit? What did you observe? What do you think about the virtual nature experience?

The Sound of Water

Each of us begins life in the watery environment of our mother's womb. It's no surprise that we're drawn to water in its many forms:

- The ebb and flow of the ocean waves
- The roar of a mountain waterfall
- The trickle of a stream's journey over rocks
- The lapping of waves against the lakeshore

Water features in the waiting rooms of doctors, dentists, and other health-care providers have been shown to reduce anxiety and blood pressure readings in patients. A Japanese study showed that the sounds of a flowing creek induced changes to blood flow in the brain that are indicative of a state of relaxation.

You can intentionally bring the sounds of water into your daily life by adding a tabletop fountain in your living space. Where might you consider adding the sound of water in your home? What feelings emerge as you listen to the sound of water?

_____

_____

_____

_____

_____

_____

_____

_____

_____

Researchers have looked at the health impacts of various soundscapes. They found that birdsong reduced stress the most, while water sounds were most helpful in improving positive emotions and health outcomes.

Creepy Crawlies

Bugs—they're everywhere! Insects are the most prolific creatures on Earth, with the largest number of individuals, species, and habitats. Most of us have an aversion to bugs, especially when they are inside our homes.

But not all bugs are bad. According to Oregon State University, out of nearly one million known insect species, only 1 to 3 percent are considered pests in our gardens. And spiders, although not insects, are highly beneficial as they feed on insects that could bite you or harm houseplants.

Most homes harbor at least a few spiders. When you see one in your home, do you kill it or scoop it up and take it outside? How do you feel about sharing your environment with them?

Though not supported by scientific research, there is anecdotal evidence that peppermint oil is a repellent for spiders and other home invaders.

Listening to Nature's Night Noises

Have you ever noticed the way the world quiets at night? Or how certain distant sounds seem louder in the dark? Our sense of hearing is not nearly as directionally focused as our sense of sight. We might detect sounds behind us, far away, or coming from a source we cannot see. Listening can tell us a lot about our surroundings, including clues about the time and weather; nearby animals, birds, and bugs; natural features such as water and trees; and human activity.

What does night sound like around your home? Step outside your door or sit by an open window after dark. Close your eyes. Take a few deep, slow breaths and allow your mind to settle. Now listen, being open to what you hear. Notice what sounds first come to your attention—are they far away or close by? Pay attention to the sounds of your own body.

Take at least five minutes for this deep listening, then reflect on these questions: What are some of the unique sounds of your home place? Are there sounds you can't identify? Sounds that are familiar and comforting? Sounds that put you on alert?

Our Feathered Friends

Bird watching is an easy way to connect with the natural world right outside your window. Because of their ability to fly, birds bring wild nature into even the most domesticated settings.

If you're new to birding, start by investigating the most common species in your region. Learning about the other living beings with whom we share our space can deepen our sense of belonging and foster a sense of place.

Attracting birds is as simple as setting up a bird feeder or a birdbath in a location you can observe from a window. Home-and-garden stores, feed stores, and pet shops often sell birdseed that is blended for the birds that frequent the region where you live.

Field guides to birds in your area and apps such as eBird and Merlin can be helpful with bird identification. If you want to observe birds up close, a pair of binoculars or the zoom feature on your camera phone can make bird behavior come alive!

ROBINS can hear earthworms move beneath the ground's surface, allowing them to snatch them up for a meal.

BALD EAGLES and other birds of prey have eyesight that is four to eight times greater than the eyesight of humans.

What are five types of birds that are common in your area?

1. _____

2. _____

3. _____

4. _____

5. _____

What would you like to explore further about our feathered friends? What do you find most fascinating about birds?

_____

_____

_____

_____

_____

_____

_____

_____

_____

_____

_____

Most HUMMING-BIRDS weigh less than an ounce, yet they can fly 1,200 miles in migration each year.

_____

_____

_____

_____

_____

CROWS can solve intricate puzzles and recognize human faces, and they are the only non-primates that can make tools.

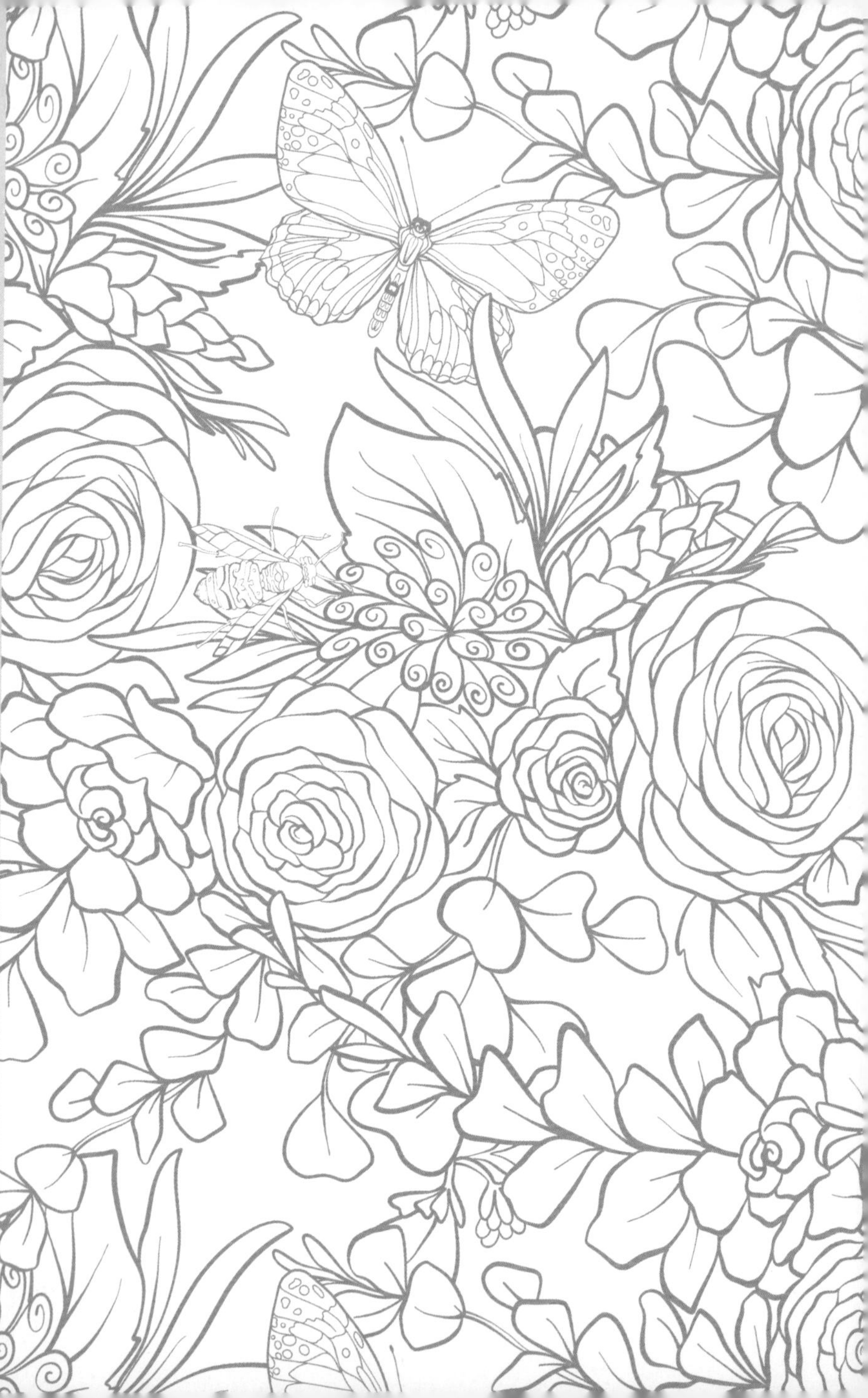

"Earth laughs
in flowers."

—Ralph Waldo Emerson,
author of "Hamatreya"

Build a
Fort Indoors

When was the last time you
built a fort inside? Besides
being just plain fun, creating a
temporary indoor shelter enacts a
deep human-nature interaction pattern.
Like rabbits digging burrows and birds
building nests, humans have a primal need
for shelter. Find a place in your home where you
can build a small shelter, ideally with a view of the
outdoors. It can be as simple as hanging a sheet over a
clothesline or setting up an outdoor camping tent in the family
room. Consider adding a sleeping bag or blanket, a few pillows, a
flashlight, and whatever else makes your indoor tent feel cozy and inviting. Crawl inside and enjoy the security and intimacy of this cozy space.

Who might you invite into your tent? A child? A partner? A pet? A friend? Or does this feel like a personal space just for you? Do you have memories of building a shelter as a child?

Capturing Nature's Beauty

Over time, repeated viewing of a favorite spot from your home or visiting a beloved tree in your neighborhood can help you feel grounded and promote a sense of place.

Try taking a photo of your special spot or tree at times when it is most beautiful. Take at least six photos of that same spot to capture its life for a year. Note below the changes it's been through.

_____

_____

_____

_____

_____

_____

_____

_____

_____

_____

_____

_____

_____

_____

_____

_____

_____

_____

What parallels do you see in the photos and in your own life during the course of the year?

_____

_____

_____

_____

_____

_____

_____

_____

_____

_____

_____

_____

_____

_____

_____

_____

_____

_____

_____

**You might consider printing and
framing the photos you created.**

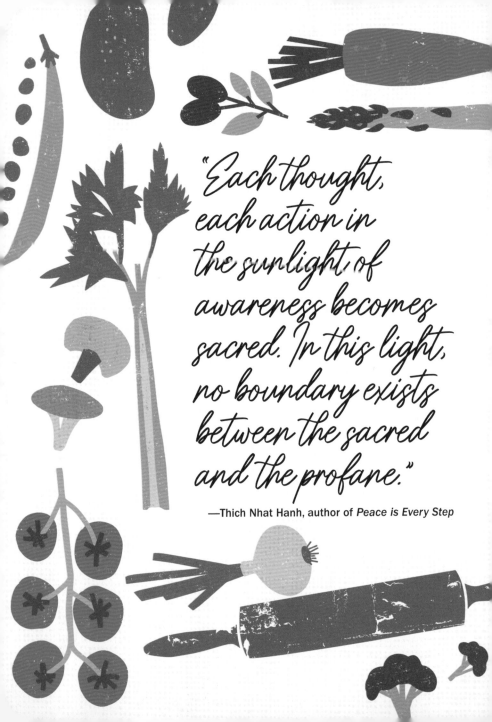

"Each thought, each action in the sunlight of awareness becomes sacred. In this light, no boundary exists between the sacred and the profane."

—Thich Nhat Hanh, author of *Peace is Every Step*

Cooking as a Sensual, Sacred Art

Preparing delicious, nourishing food from nature's bounty is a deeply sensual act. Many of our senses are stimulated by the process, including:

· The aromas wafting from the pan
· The sizzle as the food cooks
· The beauty of the nicely presented plate
· The texture of the food in our mouth
· The taste of each flavorful bite on the palette

Do you have a favorite meal that you like to prepare? Do you grow any of your ingredients? What is one thing you can do to be more intentional about cooking and enjoying food with those you love?

_____

_____

_____

_____

_____

_____

_____

Basking in the Sun

Basking in the warm rays of our solar system's
star is relaxing and often healthy in small doses. The
sun's rays cause our bodies to produce vitamin D, which
aids in the absorption of calcium, boosts our mood, strengthens
the immune system, and lowers our risk for depression, among
other benefits. Find a sunny spot where you're comfortable. It
might be indoors where the sun is streaming through a window or
outdoors in your backyard or on your deck or patio. Depending on
your location, the time of day, and the season, the sun's intensity will
vary. Notice how the sun's rays feel on your skin. If you're outdoors,
notice how the air feels as well. Is it moist with humidity or dry?
If it is chilly, notice how the cool air contrasts with the warm
sun. Looking straight ahead, open your eyes and notice
what draws your attention. Are other beings—birds,
bugs, dogs, or cats—enjoying the sun's warmth,
too? Many plants move their leaves and
flower heads to follow the sun.

What did you notice as you basked in the sun? What does the sun provide that you're most grateful for?

Exercise caution when sunbathing. Be sure to limit your time for this activity, wear appropriate sun protection, and never look directly at the sun.

Soaking Your Feet

Our feet work hard every day—supporting our weight, helping us balance, and moving us forward over varied terrain. They are often neglected and rarely appreciated as a sensual part of the body, with more nerve endings per square inch than any other part of the body.

Treat your toes to a relaxing foot soak. Feeling the water swirling around your feet is similar to some of the experiences we have in nature, like wading at the beach. Fill a basin with hot water and steep some chamomile tea in it for a soothing scent. Lower the lights and perhaps light a candle. Have a fluffy towel ready. Put on your favorite music. Once the water has cooled to warm, immerse your feet in the basin.

Notice the warmth of the water on the soles of your feet. Wiggle your toes. Feel the warm water lap around your ankles. Give yourself a few moments to relax. Sip a glass of wine, herbal tea, or your favorite beverage. Imagine the muscles in your feet softening as you soak.

My Time and Life Satisfaction

As seasons pass, we become more mindful of the finite nature of all life, including our own. The preciousness of each day comes more into focus as time slips by. How much satisfaction do you derive from the tasks in which you invest your time? Try the following simple exercise to help illuminate whether you are spending your time wisely.

MY TIME

Divide the circle into sections to show the approximate percentage of your time in a given week that is devoted to each of various aspects of your life (e.g., family time, couple time, work, hobby, home care, child care, self-care, gardening, cooking, etc.).

LIFE SATISFACTION

Divide the circle into sections to show what aspects of your life bring you the most satisfaction and pleasure.

What surprises you as you look at the charts? What aspects of your life bring the most satisfaction? Are there parts of your life that are taking a lot of your time but bringing little pleasure? Are you happy with the amount of time spent outdoors? Based on what you see, what changes could you make to interact more with nature?

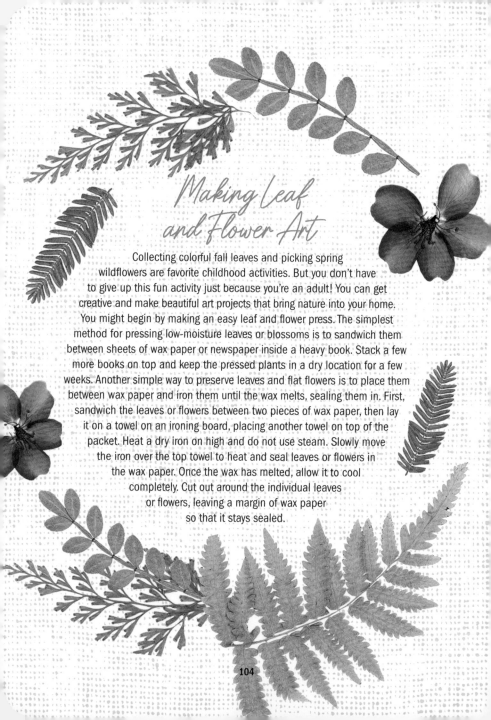

Making Leaf and Flower Art

Collecting colorful fall leaves and picking spring wildflowers are favorite childhood activities. But you don't have to give up this fun activity just because you're an adult! You can get creative and make beautiful art projects that bring nature into your home.

You might begin by making an easy leaf and flower press. The simplest method for pressing low-moisture leaves or blossoms is to sandwich them between sheets of wax paper or newspaper inside a heavy book. Stack a few more books on top and keep the pressed plants in a dry location for a few weeks. Another simple way to preserve leaves and flat flowers is to place them between wax paper and iron them until the wax melts, sealing them in. First, sandwich the leaves or flowers between two pieces of wax paper, then lay it on a towel on an ironing board, placing another towel on top of the packet. Heat a dry iron on high and do not use steam. Slowly move the iron over the top towel to heat and seal leaves or flowers in the wax paper. Once the wax has melted, allow it to cool completely. Cut out around the individual leaves or flowers, leaving a margin of wax paper so that it stays sealed.

What ideas do you have for getting creative with nature's gifts?

_____

_____

_____

_____

_____

_____

_____

_____

_____

Add a dried or preserved leaf or flower to your journal.

You can use your preserved treasures in countless ways. Here are a few suggestions: Make a wreath for your door. • Glue them around the edge of a mirror. • Use them as a centerpiece for your table. • Frame them for pretty wall art.

Bring Nature's Colors and Beauty Inside

Our homes have changed from places where we eat, sleep, and escape from the world to places where we also engage in our work, take classes, and socialize on online forums. Technology that brought these changes has made our lives easier, but it has also created new challenges, including how we think about our living space and the amount of time we spend in it.

Intentionally bringing natural elements into a space, or biophilic design, is increasingly being used in health-care settings, offices, and schools. You can do the same in your home by considering the natural light in a room, the colors you choose for the walls and flooring, the textures you incorporate, and the natural elements you use to decorate.

Is there a space in your home that you would like to infuse with more nature? One way to bring the outdoors in is to incorporate the nature that surrounds your home. For example, if you live by the ocean, you might use the colors of the water and the beach for the walls and furniture, have sheer window coverings to allow for maximum light, and include shells and sea glass in your decorating.

You might choose to incorporate nature that reminds you of a favorite place.

What is one new design element you are considering for your home?

Are You Feeling Ecoanxiety?

The internet allows us to see how climate change is affecting the planet, from the disappearance of glaciers and the increase in raging storms, to more frequent droughts and wildfires. Many of us have experienced climate-related events directly.

Some people report that they feel anxious about the health of the planet but believe that others don't share their concerns. This can lead to feeling isolated and even more anxious.

What concerns do you have about the interconnection between your health and well-being and the health of the Earth?

_____

_____

What is one thing you can do to feel more empowered to address your concerns? For example, joining a national advocacy group or a local environmental group can offer opportunities to get involved in developing solutions.

_____

_____

Talking with trusted friends and family members about your concerns might invite them to share their feelings as well and break that sense of isolation.

Who do you talk to about these concerns?

_____

_____

"Unless someone like you cares a whole awful lot, nothing is going to get better. It's not."

—Dr. Seuss, author of *The Lorax*

Befriend a Tree

Do you have a favorite tree that is visible from your home or in your neighborhood or at a nearby park? A tree can be a steady presence during uncertain times. Befriending a tree connects us with something bigger and vaster than ourselves; it can also help decrease stress, anxiety, and inflammation and foster empathy and compassion, which can improve our relationships.

If you don't have one, find a tree friend! Spend some time with "your" tree. Notice how it feels to sit with it. Feel its bark and roots. Smell it. Notice the birds and critters it's housing. Look up into its branches and at the sky above. Think about all that tree has been through—the years, the seasons, the weather conditions it has withstood—to remind you of your own strength and resilience.

Write about your tree.

_____

_____

_____

_____

_____

_____

_____

_____

_____

_____

_____

_____

My Special Nature Object

Do you have a rock, shell, feather, or other natural object that holds a special meaning? It might remind you of a time in nature when you experienced a sense of awe or a deep connection to a place. Or it might conjure memories of a special trip or time with a loved one. Find your special nature object. Hold it for a moment and think about what makes it special to you.

What is the story surrounding your special nature object? Where was it collected? Is there someone connected to that object? What do you feel as you recall its story?

Evening Meditation

The setting sun can look different, depending upon where you are located, the time of year, and the weather conditions. The changing wavelengths of light might cause the sun to look like a fiery golden ball melting into the ocean, a pink glow illuminating layers of clouds, or just a quiet disappearance of light beneath the horizon.

Find a place where you can experience the sunset. Notice the sounds of the evening growing quiet. Feel the air cool on your skin. What do you smell? Observe the changing colors of the sky as the sun slips away. Notice what you feel as another day of your life draws to a close.

Sunset is a powerful time to journal about closing chapters in your life, taking stock of where you are, and experiencing gratitude for the gift of another day.

Questions to ask yourself during your evening meditation: What is something that is holding you back? What do you need to do to let it go? What do you want to do differently tomorrow?

_____

_____

_____

_____

_____

_____

_____

_____

_____

_____

_____

_____

_____

_____

_____

What Is Your Resilience Style?

Resilience refers to our ability to recover from or adjust to change, trauma, or misfortune. One way to consider our resilience is to compare it to how different trees weather the storms and other challenges throughout their lifetimes.

One form of resilience is flexibility. The palm tree has a supple trunk and flexible leaves that allow it to be whipped around by strong winds without breaking.

Another form of resilience relies on core strength. The oak tree uses its shear strength and size to stand stalwart in a storm.

Resilience is also fostered by community and connection. The aspen's root system intertwines with the other aspen trees in the grove, supporting one another through storms.

Finally, another form of resilience is adaptability. The coastal cypress has a distinctive profile that is shaped by the winds it grows in.

What is your resilience style? What tree do you most identify with? Write about a situation where you drew on this resilience style to get you through a challenge.

_____

_____

_____

_____

_____

_____

_____

_____

_____

_____

_____

_____

Draw your tree of resilience.

Discover Your Totem

A totem is a spirit being, sacred object, or symbol of a tribe, clan, family, or individual. It often serves as an emblem or a reminder of ancestry.

Totems capture the symbolic essence of an animal, another living being, or natural phenomenon. We often associate totems with some Native American cultures, but the concept has been known throughout the world and is referenced in Greek mythology. Today, some people identify with a totem that came to them by a serendipitous experience in nature or through a dream. Others might feel a connection to an animal or plant that shares their characteristics or reminds them of home.

Do you have an animal or nature totem? If so, what is it? How did your totem come to you?

_____

_____

_____

_____

_____

_____

_____

_____

_____

_____

_____

_____

If you don't have a totem, try to figure out what yours might be. Are you particularly drawn to an animal or other being without being able to explain why? Have you ever had a recurring dream about a certain animal or being, or did you have a childhood dream that stayed with you?

_____

_____

_____

_____

_____

_____

_____

_____

_____

_____

_____

_____

_____

_____

_____

_____

_____

_____

Reciprocity

A strong sense of nature connectedness refers to feeling a bond or emotional attachment to the natural world. Research shows that the quality of our relationship with nature contributes to its impact on our health and well-being. There are many ways we can develop our connectedness with nature, including activities that stimulate our senses and feelings of compassion and a sense of belonging.

Not surprisingly, people with strong nature connectedness are more likely to engage in pro-environmental behaviors. These can include recycling, being mindful of energy and fossil-fuel usage, and participating in community restoration or cleanup projects. It may also mean fostering a love and respect for nature in their children and advocating for the environment that they love.

Giving back to nature can take many forms. What is something you're doing now that gives back to nature?

_____

_____

_____

_____

_____

_____

_____

_____

What else could you do to help care for the nature you love?

"We must somehow find the means to move beyond experiencing nature as a marginal reality reflected in the occasional visit to a park or some faraway place to making it an integral and essential part of our everyday lives."

—Stephen R. Kellert, author of *Birthright*

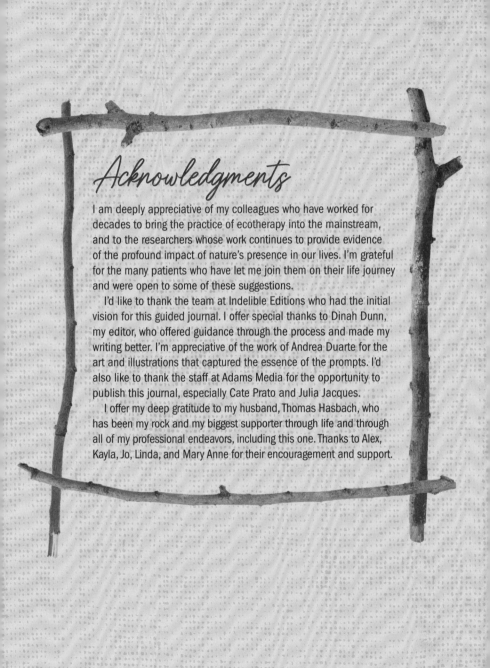

Acknowledgments

I am deeply appreciative of my colleagues who have worked for decades to bring the practice of ecotherapy into the mainstream, and to the researchers whose work continues to provide evidence of the profound impact of nature's presence in our lives. I'm grateful for the many patients who have let me join them on their life journey and were open to some of these suggestions.

I'd like to thank the team at Indelible Editions who had the initial vision for this guided journal. I offer special thanks to Dinah Dunn, my editor, who offered guidance through the process and made my writing better. I'm appreciative of the work of Andrea Duarte for the art and illustrations that captured the essence of the prompts. I'd also like to thank the staff at Adams Media for the opportunity to publish this journal, especially Cate Prato and Julia Jacques.

I offer my deep gratitude to my husband, Thomas Hasbach, who has been my rock and my biggest supporter through life and through all of my professional endeavors, including this one. Thanks to Alex, Kayla, Jo, Linda, and Mary Anne for their encouragement and support.

About the Author

A pioneer in the practice of ecotherapy, PATRICIA H. HASBACH, PhD, is a licensed psychotherapist, consultant, author, and college educator. In private practice for nearly thirty years, Dr. Hasbach specializes in managing anxiety and depression, as well as fostering health and wellness. She consults with hospitals, schools, businesses, and correctional facilities. Dr. Hasbach has served as the co-director of the Ecopsychology Certificate program in the Graduate School of Education and Counseling at Lewis & Clark College, and she sits on the editorial board of the academic journal *Ecopsychology*.

Dr. Hasbach has published numerous articles and is an author and co-editor of two MIT Press books: *The Rediscovery of the Wild* (2013) and *Ecopsychology: Science, Totems, and the Technological Species* (2012), which was nominated for the 2014 Grawemeyer Award for Psychology. Dr. Hasbach is one of the media's go-to ecotherapists, and her work has appeared in numerous outlets including *Time* magazine, *Vogue*, *Outside* magazine, *Utne Reader*, *The New York Times Magazine*, *The Wall Street Journal*, *The Christian Science Monitor*, and *Sierra* magazine.

In her free time, she enjoys hiking, kayaking, gardening, and quiet time in nature. She is an avid traveler and lover of the wild. She lives with her husband and two dogs on the McKenzie River in Eugene, Oregon.

Tim Lewis Photography